Date: 7/17/20

J 617.89 VEN
Ventura, Marne,
Hearing devices /

ENGINEERING THE HUMAN BODY

HEARING DEVICES

by Marne Ventura

FOCUS READERS

NAVIGATOR

WWW.FOCUSREADERS.COM

Focus Readers is distributed by North Star Editions:
sales@northstareditions.com | 888-417-0195

Produced for Focus Readers by Red Line Editorial.

Content Consultant: Joshua M. Alexander, PhD, CCC-A, Associate Professor of Speech, Language, and Hearing Sciences, Purdue University

Photographs ©: FatCamera/iStockphoto, cover, 1; Tempura/iStockphoto, 4–5; Gannet77/iStockphoto, 7; M.F.A.M. Museum/Shutterstock Images, 9; kurhan/Shutterstock Images, 10–11; ericsphotography/iStockphoto, 13; Srisakorn/iStockphoto, 15; Jean-Paul Chassenet/Science Source, 16–17; Rolphus/iStockphoto, 19; Robert Przybysz/Shutterstock Images, 21; Arno Massee/Science Source, 23; Pavel_D/Shutterstock Images, 24–25; Dragon Images/Shutterstock Images, 27; SPL/Science Source, 29

Library of Congress Cataloging-in-Publication Data
Names: Ventura, Marne, author.
Title: Hearing devices / by Marne Ventura.
Description: Lake Elmo, MN : Focus Readers, [2020] | Series: Engineering the human body | Audience: Grades 4 to 6. | Includes bibliographical references and index.
Identifiers: LCCN 2018054457 (print) | LCCN 2018058969 (ebook) | ISBN 9781641859738 (pdf) | ISBN 9781641859042 (e-book) | ISBN 9781641857666 (hardcover) | ISBN 9781641858359 (pbk.)
Subjects: LCSH: Hearing aids--Juvenile literature. | Hearing--Juvenile literature. | Hearing aids--Technological innovations--Juvenile literature.
Classification: LCC RF300 (ebook) | LCC RF300 .V465 2020 (print) | DDC 617.89--dc23
LC record available at https://lccn.loc.gov/2018054457

Printed in the United States of America
Mankato, MN
May, 2019

ABOUT THE AUTHOR

Marne Ventura is the author of nearly 80 books for kids. A former elementary school teacher, she holds a master's degree in education from the University of California. Her favorite topics are science, history, arts and crafts, food, and the lives of creative people. Marne and her husband live on the central coast of California.

TABLE OF CONTENTS

CHAPTER 1

JAKE'S STORY

Jake is an excellent drummer. He started playing drums when he was five years old. He attended the Arts Academy in Philadelphia, Pennsylvania. Jake was also a member of the All-City Philadelphia Orchestra. This youth orchestra is for talented middle school and high school students.

Both children and adults can be diagnosed with hearing loss.

When Jake was three years old, his family became concerned about his hearing. An **audiologist** diagnosed Jake with hearing loss in both ears. Jake started wearing hearing aids. They helped at first.

Jake loves music. But his hearing kept getting worse. Eventually, Jake could not hear even with his hearing aids. When he was nine years old, doctors placed a cochlear **implant** in his left ear. When Jake was 13 years old, he had another surgery. Doctors put a cochlear implant in his right ear.

The implants helped. Jake could hear many sounds he couldn't hear before.

Part of a cochlear implant rests on the patient's outer ear. The rest is placed inside the body.

He could hear the instruments in the orchestra. He could hear birds singing.

People of all ages can lose their hearing. And there are many causes of hearing loss. Some people are born with the condition. The cause is often **genetic**.

Other people lose their hearing. Loud noises or diseases can cause hearing loss in children and adults. Sometimes, the loss is temporary. Other times, it is permanent.

Engineers make hearing devices to help people with hearing loss. Hearing aids are

EAR TRUMPETS

Before the invention of modern hearing aids, people with hearing loss used ear trumpets. These devices were often small and horn shaped. People held the narrow end in their ear canal. They pointed the wide end of the device toward the sound they wanted to hear. The wide end sent sound into the ear canal. The ear trumpet made the sound louder. It also blocked out other sounds in the background.

People began using ear trumpets in the 1700s to help with hearing loss.

devices that make sounds louder. Some hearing aids fit on the back of the ear. Others are placed in the outer ear or the ear canal. Implants are hearing devices that are placed surgically. Thanks to hearing devices, people with hearing loss can hear the world around them.

CHAPTER 2

HEARING AND HEARING LOSS

The human ear has three parts. They all play a role in hearing. The outer ear is the part that can be seen. Its shape helps collect sound waves. It funnels sound through the ear canal to the second part of the ear.

The middle ear contains the eardrum and three tiny bones called ossicles.

To better hear, people might cup their hands around their outer ears.

The ossicles are the smallest bones in the human body. Sound waves reach the eardrum. The eardrum moves. Its movement makes the ossicles move, too. These bones move in a way that makes sound louder. Their movement sends **vibrations** into the third part of the ear.

The inner ear, or cochlea, is shaped like a snail. It is filled with fluid. It also has thousands of tiny hair cells. Some of these cells make the vibrations stronger. Other cells respond to the vibrations. They send electrical messages to the **auditory nerve**. This nerve sends the messages to the brain. When that happens, the person hears a sound.

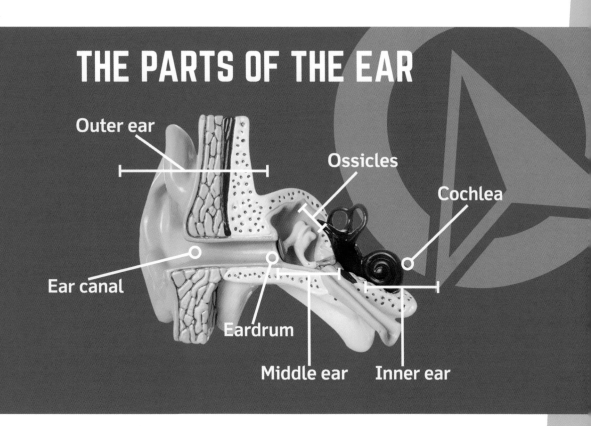

THE PARTS OF THE EAR

Outer ear

Ossicles

Cochlea

Ear canal

Eardrum

Middle ear

Inner ear

Sometimes a problem occurs during one of these steps. The problem could result in hearing loss. In some cases, sound doesn't travel very well through the outer and middle ear. This disorder is called conductive hearing loss.

A person might have fluid in the middle ear because of an ear infection. The fluid makes it difficult for the eardrum and ossicles to move. Or a person may have a hole in the eardrum. The shape of the ear canal or the bones in the middle ear can also be the cause.

Conductive hearing loss can often be fixed with medicine or surgery. When it cannot be fixed, a hearing device that moves the middle ear bones can help the person hear.

Sometimes the hair cells inside the cochlea fail to send electrical messages to the brain. This disorder is called sensorineural hearing loss. Some people

Ear infections can hurt, but they often heal on their own.

are born with hair cells that do not work.
Other people develop this type of hearing
loss because of illness or injury. Aging
can cause it, too. Sensorineural hearing
loss is permanent. Doctors usually
recommend hearing aids for this type of
hearing loss.

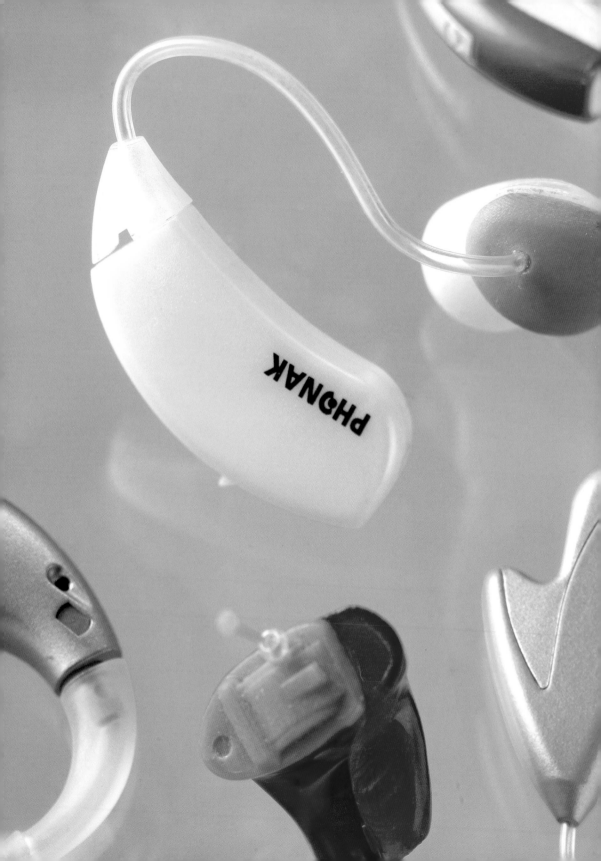

CHAPTER 3

HOW HEARING AIDS WORK

Engineers have designed several types of hearing aids to help people with hearing loss. These removable devices work by making sound waves bigger.

Hearing aids have four basic parts. A microphone picks up sound waves and turns them into electrical signals. An amplifier makes the signals stronger.

Hearing aids come in many styles. Patients work with audiologists to find the right styles for them.

A receiver turns the signals back into sound waves. Then it sends the sound waves into the ear canal. Finally, a battery gives the hearing aid energy to work.

One kind of hearing aid fits inside the ear canal. It is small and hard to see. And it does not pick up as much background wind noise as other styles.

A second kind of hearing aid fits into the outer ear. A button on the aid allows users to adjust the volume to make sounds louder or softer. These aids can **amplify** sound more than those that fit in the ear canal. They are also more visible.

Behind-the-ear hearing aids are a third type. They curve over the top of the outer

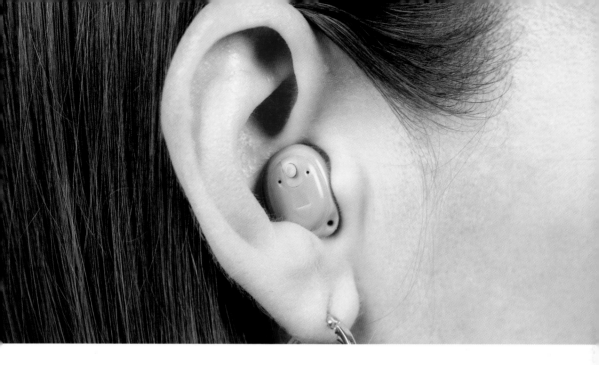

An audiologist can design a custom hearing aid that fits into the user's ear canal.

ear and rest behind it. Most of the hearing aids sold today are in this style.

Most hearing aids today have a computer chip. It changes sound into a **digital** signal. Using math, the chip can change the digital signal. The chip might make the signal louder or clearer.

It might even reduce background sounds. Then the chip changes the new digital signal back into sound waves the person can hear.

EXPERTS WORKING TOGETHER

Different kinds of experts work together to design hearing aids. Biomedical engineers study how the inner ear works. They find ways to solve hearing problems. Electrical engineers make circuits. These devices control the computer chips. Hearing scientists study how the brain understands sound. They use the knowledge of biomedical engineers. Then they tell electrical engineers how the hearing aid should change sound to help people hear better. Materials engineers study the best materials to use for hearing aids.

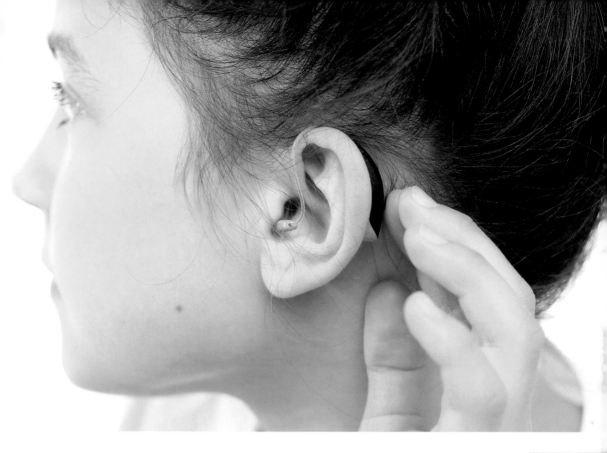

Behind-the-ear hearing aids fit into the ear canal and also curve behind the ear.

Hearing aids can help most people with hearing loss. But some people are not able to hear sounds at all. They have a condition known as profound deafness. For people with profound deafness, cochlear implants can be helpful.

COCHLEAR IMPLANTS

A cochlear implant has three parts. The first part sits behind the ear. It has a microphone and a computer chip called a speech processor. The second part is an implant. A surgeon places this part under the skin behind the ear. The third part is a set of **electrodes** placed in the cochlea.

The microphone picks up sound. The speech processor turns the sound into a digital signal. It sends the signal to the implant. The implant changes the digital signal into electrical signals. It sends the electrical signals to the electrodes in the cochlea. The electrodes send messages directly to the nerve endings in the cochlea. The auditory nerve signals the brain. When that happens, the person hears sound.

The implant sends electrical signals from the speech processor to electrodes placed in the patient's cochlea.

Many cochlear implant users can understand speech when there is little background noise. Some can even hear on the phone. But cochlear implants are not a perfect substitute for the working ear.

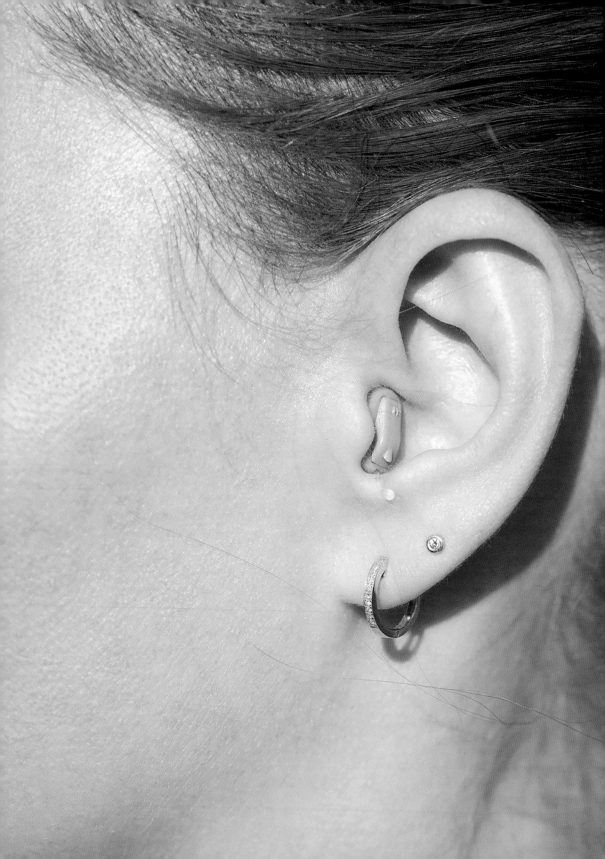

CHAPTER 4

EMERGING TECHNOLOGY

Scientists are working to improve hearing devices. They want to make hearing aids smaller, lighter, less visible, and more effective. Scientists are also looking for new ways to help users control how their hearing aids work.

Hearing aids can connect wirelessly to phones, televisions, and computers.

Through improvements in technology, hearing aids are becoming smaller and less visible.

The sound goes directly to the hearing aid. Users can control their hearing aids using apps on their phones.

Some scientists are trying to eliminate the troubles of hearing in background noise. People with hearing aids can have trouble hearing one person talk in

NANOTECHNOLOGY

Scientists who study nanotechnology make things that are very tiny. Their studies have affected hearing devices. For example, engineers have found ways to make the parts smaller. Hearing aids have gotten smaller and less visible over time. Today's devices can be as tiny as beans. In some cases, they can fit in the ear and not be seen at all.

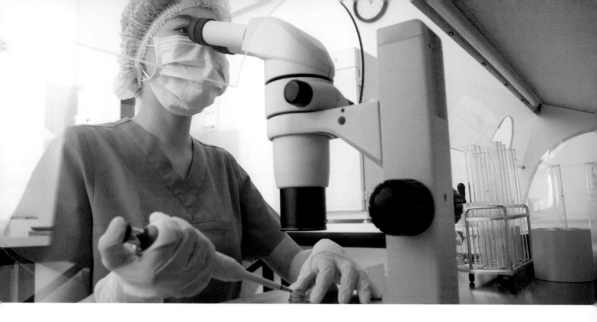

Scientists continue to research ways to restore hearing.

a noisy place. Hearing aids can reduce background noise. But they cannot pick out which talker the user wants to hear.

Scientists are working on a new device that can check the user's brain. The device will be able to tell which talker the user wants to listen to. It will be able to filter out all other sounds and amplify the talker's voice.

Other scientists are testing ways to regrow the hair cells in the cochlea. Some birds can regrow lost or damaged hair cells. But humans cannot. Scientists are using information they have learned from bird cells. They are working to create a drug that might someday help humans regrow hair cells.

Scientists have known for many years that hair cells pick up sounds and change them into electrical signals. But scientists did not know how. In 2018, researchers discovered that a specific **protein** called TMC1 turns sounds into nerve signals. A damaged or missing TMC1 protein causes hearing loss. Scientists will use

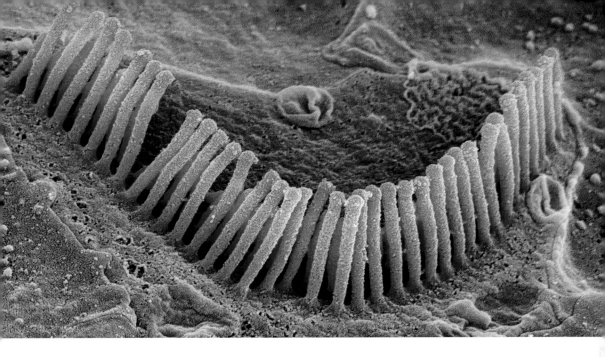

Hair cells have projections (orange) that move when vibrations enter the inner ear.

this information to work on new ways to treat people with hearing loss.

Millions of people develop hearing loss. Devices such as hearing aids and implants help them hear. Future advancements will help make sound even more accessible to people with hearing loss.

FOCUS ON
HEARING DEVICES

Write your answers on a separate piece of paper.

1. Write a sentence that describes the key ideas from Chapter 2.

2. If you had mild to moderate hearing loss, which type of hearing aid would you choose? Why?

3. Where is the cochlea located?

     A. in the outer ear
     B. in the middle ear
     C. in the inner ear

4. What would happen if a hearing aid did not have an amplifier?

     A. The hearing aid would not create electrical signals.
     B. The hearing aid would not make sounds louder.
     C. The hearing aid would pick up background noise.

Answer key on page 32.

GLOSSARY

amplify
To make something bigger or louder.

audiologist
A health-care professional who diagnoses and treats people with hearing loss.

auditory nerve
The nerve that carries sound information from the cochlea to the brain.

digital
Having to do with information used on a computer.

electrodes
Devices through which electrical signals enter or leave an area.

genetic
Relating to traits and molecules inherited from parents.

implant
A device that is placed inside the body by a surgeon.

protein
A molecule that is important in telling a living cell what to do.

vibrations
The fast movements of particles or matter.

TO LEARN MORE

BOOKS

Kenney, Karen Latchana. *Sound and Light Waves Investigations*. Minneapolis: Lerner Publications, 2018.

Sohn, Emily. *Adventures in Sound with Max Axiom, Super Scientist: An Augmented Reading Science Experience*. North Mankato, MN: Capstone Press, 2019.

Solway, Andrew. *From Crashing Waves to Music Download: An Energy Journey Through the World of Sound*. Chicago: Heinemann Raintree, 2015.

NOTE TO EDUCATORS

Visit **www.focusreaders.com** to find lesson plans, activities, links, and other resources related to this title.

INDEX